karrawirra parri

walking the torrens from source to sea

karrawirra parri

walking the torrens from source to sea

Mike Ladd

Photographs by Cathy Brooks

Wakefield Press

To Lachlan Colquhoun;

friend, editor, provocateur.

Wakefield Press
1 The Parade West
Kent Town
South Australia 5067
www.wakefieldpress.com.au

First published 2012

Designed and typeset by Mark Thomas
Printing and quality control in China by Tingleman Pty Ltd

National Library of Australia Cataloguing-in-Publication entry

Author:	Ladd, Mike, 1959– .
Title:	Karrawirra Parri: walking the Torrens from source to sea / Mike Ladd; photographs by Cathy Brooks.
ISBN:	978 1 74305 019 4 (pbk.).
Subjects:	Ladd, Mike, 1959 – Anecdotes. Australian poetry – 21st century. Torrens, River (S. Aust.) – History. Torrens, River (S. Aust.) – Social life and customs.
Other Authors/ Contributors:	Brooks, Cathy, photographer.
Dewey Number:	A821.3

Publication of this book was assisted by the Commonwealth Government through the Australia Council, its arts funding and advisory body.

Between the late autumn and early spring of 2007, I walked the river Torrens from its source to the sea, writing in my notebook as I travelled. The description of the journey was later serialised in the *Adelaide Review,* accompanied by photographs by Cathy Brooks. The complete series is published here for the first time. "Karrawirra Parri", meaning "river of the red gum forests", is the official Kaurna name for the Torrens. Taking the form of a haibun (a diary written in prose and poetry) *Karrawirra Parri* is a social and natural history of the river as well as a collection of personal observations along the way.

My thanks to the committee of the Barbara Hanrahan award and to the many people who helped me with research: Carol Hannaford, Bryce Bell, Neale Draper, Gwenda Dally, Chester Schultz, Rob Amery, Lewis O'Brien, Joe Mitchell, Lyn O'Grady and Rick Hosking.

I gratefully acknowledge the Kaurna Warra Pintyandi for permission to use the name Karrawirra Parri.

Mike Ladd

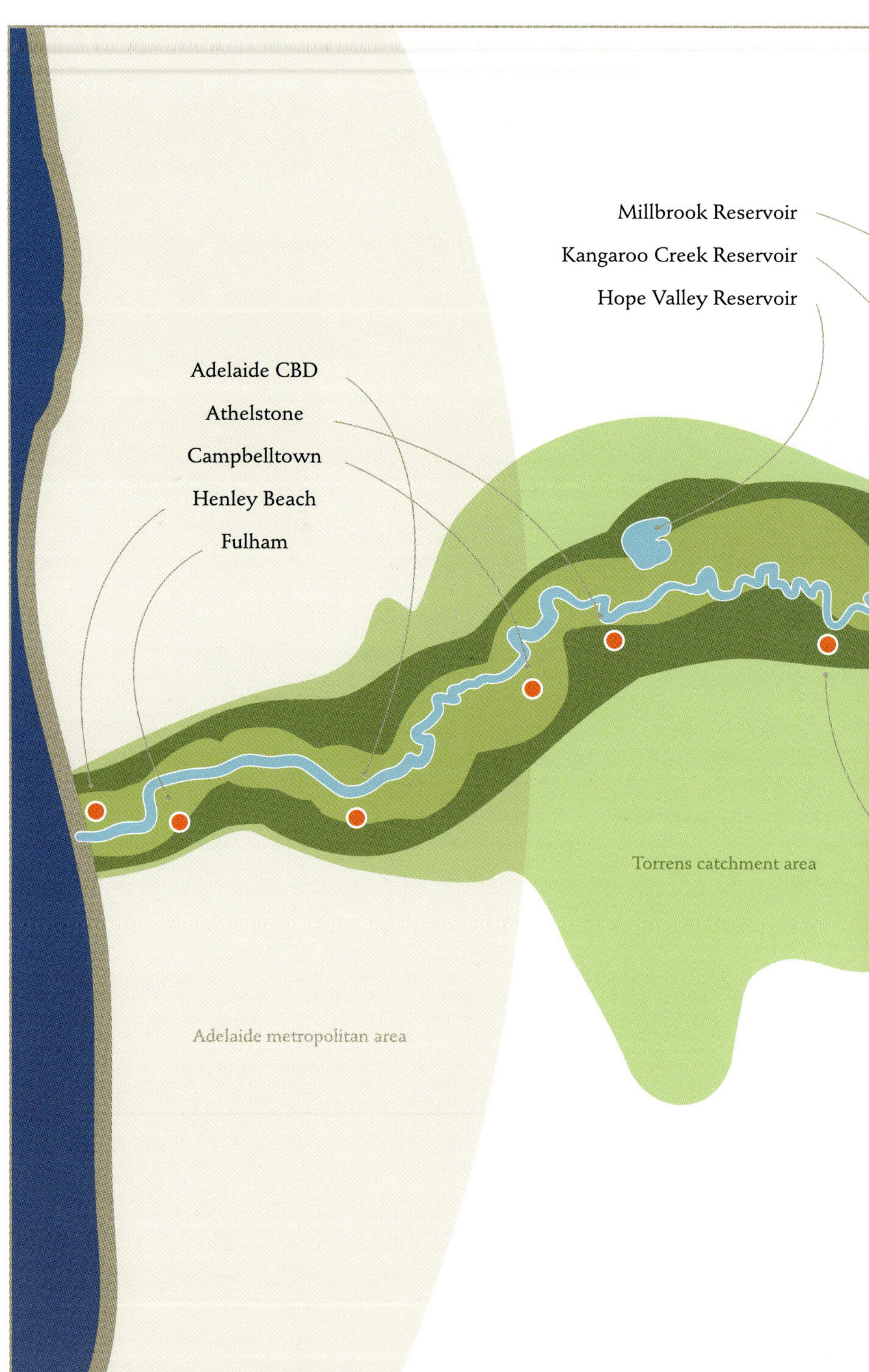

Millbrook Reservoir
Kangaroo Creek Reservoir
Hope Valley Reservoir
Adelaide CBD
Athelstone
Campbelltown
Henley Beach
Fulham
Torrens catchment area
Adelaide metropolitan area

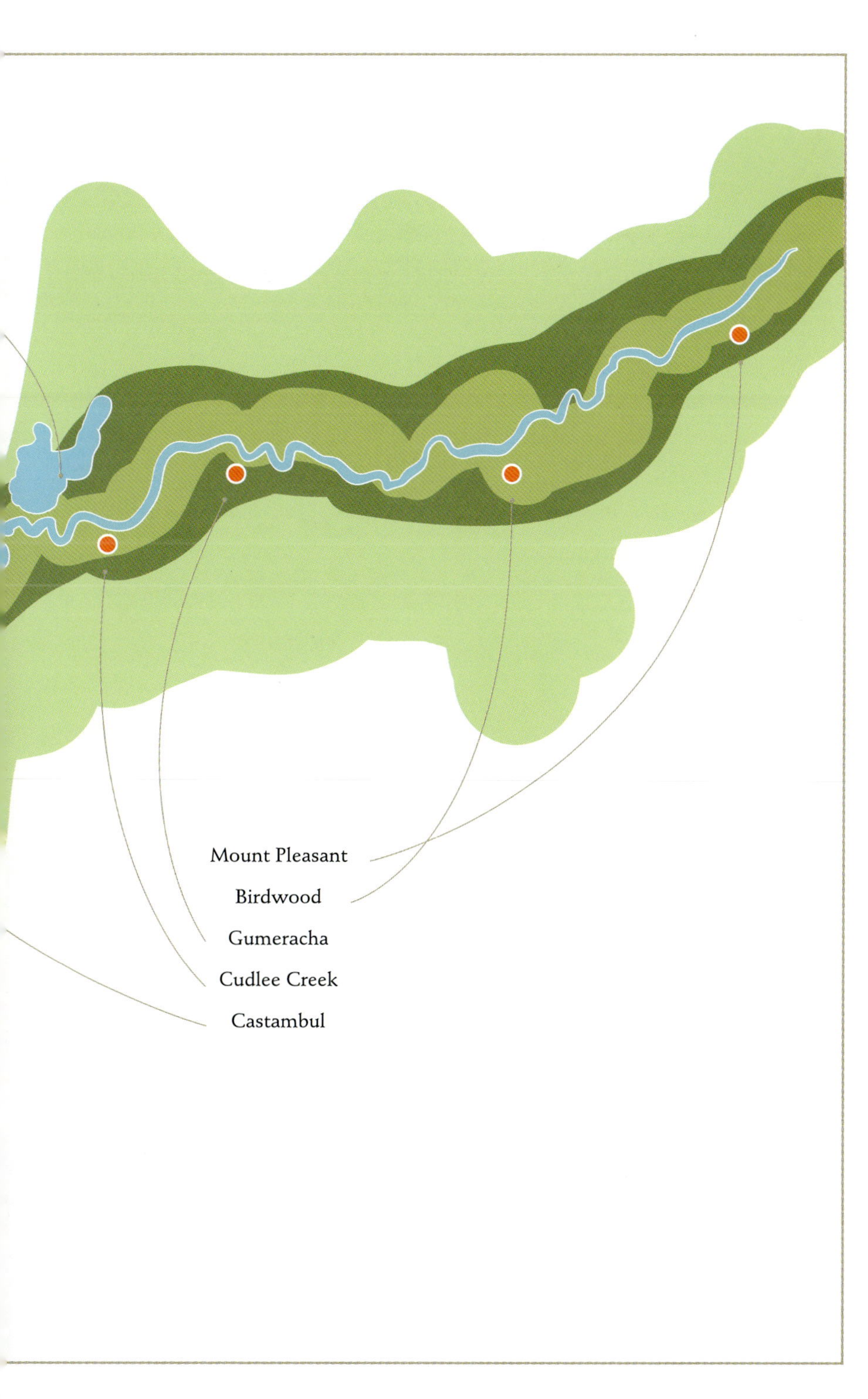
Mount Pleasant
Birdwood
Gumeracha
Cudlee Creek
Castambul

Late autumn – I start my journey here,
in this paddock on the Anderson's farm
between Springton and Mount Pleasant.
A ridge of ironstone runs east-west – from its
northern slope begins the Marne, from its southern,
the Torrens.

At last, it's raining.
Straight down – the best kind.
It feels like the world has some faith in us again.

The top of the paddock is guarded by two weighty red gums, well-seasoned in battle, scarred and twisted. From these two old soldiers, a line of trees runs southwest; the first pencil line of the river. As Stephen Anderson and I walk around the base of one of the trees, a hare startles and pounds across the paddock. Back near the farmhouse, Stephen has thousands of native seedlings growing in trays: sedges, reeds, she-oak, ti-tree, red and blue gum. With them, he and his father are revegetating their land.

The river has no childhood before it is pressed into service. It runs only 150 metres before it meets its first dam. Now, after such severe drought, it is a remnant pool in the bottom of a clay ditch. I bend to the surface, and dip in my hand. The source of a river is like the source of a language – manifold and lost in mythology. "Pegai" means "source" – Pegasus is so named because he was born near the source of the ocean. He is also associated with rain. Pegasus flew to Mount Helikon, and where he stamped his hoof, a spring was born – the Hippocrene fountain. Sacred to the muses, those who drank its water were given poetic inspiration.

There are no winged horses here – just a magpie or two, and that hare watching from the bushes. If I drink this water from the bottom of the dam I will more likely be given a bellyache than a poem. Nevertheless, I scoop a handful and drink. The water tastes of clay, eucalypt, dead beetles – and it tastes of beginnings.

As I walk southwest, following the road to Mount Pleasant, I think of my heroes, the walking poets: Basho, trudging the roads of northern Honshu, his shoulders sore from his pack; Wordsworth, muttering to himself, striding along the edges of ditches in the Lake District; and Mandelstam tramping the snow-locked streets of St Petersburg and then later pacing his prison cell because he couldn't keep still, the poetry coming through him

with the walking. A "foot" of verse derives from marking time with the feet. I am thinking of this as I squelch away from the source, and I feel glad to be both free in my own walking and to be a member of this archaic profession. The air is clear and cool, and the magpies are beginning their afternoon descending songs. I set out knowing roughly where I am going, but not what I'll find on the way. You raise a foot, you lower a foot.

I carry with me one small book, Basho's *Narrow Road to the Interior,* which is a model for this whole enterprise. It begins with the lines:

> The moon and the sun are eternal travellers. Even the years wander on. A lifetime adrift in a boat, or in old age leading a tired horse into the years, every day is a journey, and the journey itself is home.

A car hisses past at 110. After the Anderson's farm, any trace of a river seems to have vanished, except for drainage lines crossing back and forth under the road. Before long, another dam, ever larger, appears. Black-headed wood ducks stare from the dam rim down into its low, pipe-clay water.

This is Peramangk country, and perhaps they had a story for this river, much older than Hesiod or Pegasus. As I pass red gums with their bases hollowed out, I think of families wintering in these shelters, their bodies wrapped in possum fur, the smoke from their fires curling up inside the great black chimneys of the eucalypts.

It is said the forest and hill-dwelling Peramangk were feared by the plains peoples and vice versa. They had opposite tastes in horizons; but they traded with each other. The Peramangk exchanged tool-making quartz, possum skins and good canoe bark, for the light whippy spear-shafts of mallee brought to them by the Lake Alexandrina tribes, the Portaulun and the Jarildekald. They also traded fire-making flint and pyrites with the Kaurna and visited them on the plains for ceremony.

The Peramangk originally thought the colonists were the ghosts of their own people, but the ghosts stayed, and the Peramangk were swiftly pushed out from this prime land in the hills. Some of their descendants now live in Mannum and Nildottie on the Murray. They left their rock paintings throughout the Mount Lofty Ranges and traces of their language survive – "Kuitpo" means a sacred or forbidden place. Now I, a descendant of the "ghosts", walk through a gloomy section of trees, and I can't help but think of absences, an emptiness that haunts the forests.

Quartz and bone in the river bed.
The Peramangk became ghosts
to the white ghosts of their dead.

The Peramangk told the European settlers that in this part of the world there was a twelve year cycle; seven years of drought, followed by five of rain. I hope they were right; it's been dry since 2000.

The source of a river is not just the drain lines and little creeks sketched in blue on the maps – but a whole geology. Sediment from a thousand-million year old sea was formed into rock and pushed up five hundred million years ago to create these ranges. Ground by ice, faulted and tilted, they were worn down to make the source hills of the ancestral river, slowing winding to a further-off sea.

The river forms the ocean,
the ocean forms the river.

At Lone Elk Road, a farm dog barks at me, startling me back from the Precambrian to now. Milk churn letterboxes wait at the corner. No-one else walks this road, though occasional cars swish past. I think of a poem by Wang Chien, over a thousand years old:

> The mountain villages bear river-names,
> Poisonous mists rise from damp sands,
> Strange fires gleam through the night rain
> And no-one passes but the lonely seeker
> of pearls.

I am optimistic, heartened to think that Wang Chien can be known to me across centuries, continents, politics and languages. A thought strikes me that makes me smile, though I smile to no-one but myself as I head towards Mount Pleasant:

There have been many thousand-year poems,
but there has never been a thousand-year reich.

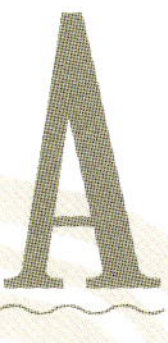
white-naped honeyeater
fluffed out against the cold
subtle in its olives and greys,
falls silent. I approach a stone well.

Now I see another sign of a stream bed and yet another dam. Nailed to a gum tree beside the road are three name plates: "Paul", "Jars" and "Jack". "DAD" in wrought iron above a white cross. Plastic flowers, a stubby holder and a Port Power doll are fixed to the trunk. Some local boys misjudged the bend one December night and became this roadside memorial. I pause to read, then move on.

Death is married to life,
but life prefers to look single.

In a field on the other side of the road, alpacas stand watching, long-necked and still. A baby alpaca squeals; an Andean voice in these South Australian hills. We never stop mixing things up. We are seed bearers, gene scatterers, pox carriers, life messengers, doom bringers, language borrowers. We ourselves are a soup of hybridity.

Past Partalunga Vineyard, where an elegant house stands amongst stone paths and garden walls fired

with ivy, the creek bed reappears, crossing under the road through a culvert. There is still no water, but green sedges and grass grow in the bed and there is the welcome sound of a frog. Then I come across the first pool, motionless and black. Coarse moss, lime-green Axminster, grows on grey concrete.

Near where a tributary winds in from the northwest is a perfect shelter tree. I stand in its charcoal-lined cave, looking out at the new green in sharp cloud-strobed light. In a circle at the tree's base are field mushrooms, a hand and a half wide. Tip them over and smell autumn earth. There are fungi everywhere, as if their indefatigable cells baked a million cakes in the night. Gold tops as well. Eat those and you'll hear the trees speak with a human voice.

Everywhere too, I see signs of the Upper Torrens Landcare Project and its plantings, reclaiming the banks and the watercourses with corridors of native trees and grasses. This gives me some hope, not only for the river, but for this project of mine. I mean, why write a rambling pastorale in the beginning of the twenty first century? Who cares about a modest journey along a local creek, when the world eats itself with smog and waste and war? Perhaps it is a word-replanting, insignificant when compared to the riparian, but still, it repairs something in me.

In the swamp behind the golf-course
a marble frog sings happiness.
More rain coming.

In the distance I see a black marker and a red, then come to another roadside memorial. Faded plastic flowers and rusty fence-wire spelling "TYE" on the trunk of a blue gum.

On the other side of the road, the sound of a chainsaw comes across the paddock where two men cut at a storm-fallen tree, twice the size of their truck.

Three brown horses stand, freeze-framed, at Amber Glen.

I pass the fine, layered stone work of Kent Farm, smell the kitchen smoke from Nyari – to my hungry nose the sharp wood smell says "dinner" as well as fire.

The river winds in to Totness. Bulrushes and sedges and dark pools beside Henry Giles's old flour mill.

A smell inside of hay bales and lanolin, slat floors
and heavy beams in decaying light – imported trees:
willow, ash and poplar, occupy the creek.

I call at a stranger's house,
asking for local history.
A cobweb on the doorbell.

Roast beef and dark ale for dinner at the front
counter of the Talunga pub. The Friday night raffle
is in progress over the noise of the Crows' game
on television. Trays of meat, six packs of beer,
truncheons of mettwurst are claimed by the winners.
In the swirl of the raffle, I talk to a guy named Andy
who claims he went down the Torrens on a boogie
board all the way from here to Birdwood.

Later, when the game is over and my end of the
bar is empty, the publican tells me his wife left him
with their three kids just a couple of days before
Christmas. Shot through with one of his customers.
His girls help work the bar and clean the rooms. The
three-piece band in the almost-deserted performance
space next to the bar plays a cover of Green Day.
The publican's oldest daughter says she loves this
one, and sings the words "I hope you have the time
of your life". She'll be eighteen soon, and I hope that

she does. The publican offers me a glass of port on the house. In these pubs, port comes from a barrel and is served in brimming pony glasses. And then it's good night.

At Mount Pleasant, in the dull autumn leaves of plane trees, I watch the orange and blue life of rosellas. I love this evolutionary speciality of place that makes rosellas yellow in the Murray lands, crimson in the eastern forests, and orange here. That gives a certain grasshopper two bands on its abdomen in one range and three in the next. It satisfies me as much as any religion, without the need to look for anything "beyond".

Wind and misty rain – magpies joust and sing contest songs for nesting sites.

Read in a shop window as I leave town:

> Wanted: Land. Just to chew the grass.
> Wanted: Chess partner, anywhere in the region.
> For Sale: Shirt and jumper.
> Message underneath: I'm interested in the jumper.

I walk on past the ritual combat ground (the football oval) behind which the permanent caravan people live. Poverty forms a bedraggled line of annexes and lean-tos by the creek, which here grows wider, with steeper eroded banks. Exposed tree roots and rusted fence lines hang over deeper black pools.

The flow becomes visible. The stream forms oxbows and small anabranches. With boyish pleasure I scatter a grey herd of sheep across green pasture. Wind stirs the reed beds and the clouds go flying. Squalls of rain rattle on my coat hood.

It is difficult to follow rivers in this world of private property. Fences, locked gates, and electric wires cut me off, force me away from free gravity-defined meandering onto the straight roads of quotidian human traffic. Intermittently, I must crunch along the verge. I come to yet another roadside memorial, a Holden Gemini badge nailed to the cross:

> R.I.P. TUBZ
> Flat out sideways man!
> Forever young.

At Brookwood I hear what sounds like a waterfall or sea surge. A pipeline comes over the hills from the east. Emerging from a pretty run through white-limbed trees and reed-fringed pools, the little Torrens gets a very rude shove. Big Brother Murray crashes into it from the pipeline's outlet, giving it a mighty bum's rush. Suddenly there's current, flow, splash and rumble, and the water turns a milky jade-green. I follow it, infected with new energy myself, through lichen-covered rocks sparkling with mica, climbing on the rims of small sandstone cliffs at the bends, and down again through spiky vegetation, where weebills chirp, hidden in the yellow gorse.

In 1839, somewhere not far from here, the ornithologist John Gould shot a bittern in an overflow pool. The bird lives in a print now, with its yellow mask, slicked-back crest, and bib of delicately-marked buff and black feathers, but where is its booming voice in this valley?

At Narcooma, the stream is a paragon of streams, coming through the corridor of bulrushes and ribbon gums. I spend an hour staring at arriving and departing water. The Stony Creek junction was revegetated in November 1996. In only ten years, this is how good it can look.

Near the ford at Black Snake Road, I find an old hearth with no house, not even a chimney. To me, this hollow stone rectangle tapering to a pyramid is a monument to words. Hearths are where language came from. When early humans found and controlled fire they began to sit together in circles, developing their simple hunting signals into systems capable of telling stories. To stay in close proximity

NO

they had to trust and understand each other. Each stone in a hearth is a word in a story, and often, they are the final part of the house to survive.

Hard rain begins to fall. I crawl inside a shelter tree on the bank of the river. At their burnt-out bases, these river red gums have womb openings, and they work as they have always worked. Inside I'm warm and dry while the rain comes down in gusts, shivering the leaves above.

Childhood cubby, foetal bliss –
a grey-haired man
in the tree's core
listens to the rain.

There is a delicious irony here. Nailed to the trunk above me is a grey tin sign: "Private property. No Entry." I inspect the cobwebs on the charcoal ceiling, eat bread and cheese for lunch, while the rain clouds pass.

Past Codger's Creek, the walking is difficult, through thigh-high couch grass, reed beds and swamps.

Over the swirling pool
the rope-swing of summer
hangs by a thread.

The river winds in under the Birdwood Hills – or perhaps "Blumberg" Hills. This town changed its name in the First World War, just as the North and South Rhine became the Somme and the Marne. In the future, I hope this body of water I'm following will be called by its Kaurna name again: "Karrawirra Parri", "river of the red gum forests".

On top of Blumberg Hill is a microwave relay station, a site sacred to our holy of holies – electronic communication. It is marked with a grey steel tower like a modified Cross of Lorraine. Below, the town whines its way through Saturday, the sound of someone's bandsaw carrying across the valley.

South of Birdwood, the river races through Rathjen's farm. I walk in tall bracken. Sunlight sparkles on the water as it pushes through bulrushes. On a red gum beside a broad, quiet pool is the clear incised line of a canoe: another trace of the Peramangk. Further on, in the bark of a smaller red gum, I think I can see a shield outline, cut who knows how long ago. Not everything is lost.

Kangaroo grass sways by the stream. New Holland honeyeaters dart in and out of the sunlight, from bush to bush. Fenced off from the stock, the indigenous Torrens reasserts itself: native pine, she-oak and Christmas bush, blackwood, ti-tree, and native cherry, hardenbergia, yacca, and grevillea, hop bush, hand flower and flax lily. Running postman, maidenhair fern, and water-couch array themselves along the creek.

Observed today: cormorant, blue wren, galah, grey crane, rosella, kookaburra, and high in the wintry blue, nankeen kestrel.

A long necked tortoise
beside a water-polished rock –
one a little slower than the other.

Also noted along the river: possum, western grey kangaroo, water rat, and yabby. Unseen by me, but perhaps still here: galaxias, brush-tailed phascogale and bilby.

Under Woodcutters Hill:

> The dead fox
> with his 1080 stare
> and his 1080 grin.

His coat is so fresh, he must have died last night. Such a bland name "1080", conjuring log books in laboratories – was it the scientists' one thousand and eightieth try that produced the deadliest compound, or do the numbers refer to a mixing proportion?

Coming in to Gumeracha, a name said to mean "fine waterhole" (doubtful because the language is unsourced) I see a wooden rocking horse looking over the tallest trees. It changes the scale of everything; suddenly I'm a plastic soldier on green felt. Toy cows watch from a play-set farm.

Out of the town there is the sense of the gorge beginning – pine-topped ridges and hillsides planted to olive and grape. I pass an oak with the sun behind

it, a light box of black limbs and ultimate yellow.
I am funnelled in. The river slows and broadens, held back by Gumeracha Weir.

At the weir the water is a metre and a half below the wall. Nothing coming over the stone steps – a quiet ziggurat. Downstream, the Torrens returns to its reduced self; pools connected by trickles of water.

I cross under Monfries Bridge, struggling through blackberry and gorse. The banks of the river steepen, yellow-orange sandstone on one side, grey-green scree on the other. Up ahead I can hear the river talking again, under its own gravity this time, limbering up for the race through the gorge.

Over the hill,
the moon,
a ghost.

Walking west, the clean winter sun on my face, roo tracks in the sand, the gorge walls closing in now, the stream gathering pace.

It is too steep here to walk along the river and again I'm forced onto the narrow road.
It's dangerous – blind curves, and very little room

between the edge of the bitumen and the barrier rail. No-one walks this bit. I could be smeared against the steel barrier by the speeding cars or clipped by the wing mirrors of the processions of motorbikes.

This is a favourite bikie route. They are like twenty-first-century horsemen, their steeds hitched in a line at the pubs and kiosks. Uniform in their samurai outfits of black leather and silver chains, they are called Dave and Ace and Mash and Keith and Wingnut and Ravo. Gangsters, or ordinary blokes not averse to the illusion, enjoying the changing pitch of the motor and leaning into the bends, the power and energy of the pack.

Down this hill my right knee has had enough and I limp in to the Cudlee Creek Caravan Park to rest for the night. Cudlee Creek has nothing to do with cuddles. Its name comes from the Kaurna "kadli" – "native dog" creek. This is a zone between the lands of the Peramangk and the Kaurna. The "yultiwirra", the stringybark forests of the Mount Lofty Ranges, mark the eastern boundary of the Kaurna, but in the past it was a floating and constantly negotiated border, depending on who was camping where, and which hunting parties were on the move. The "pangkarra" was family territory for hunting and gathering, but the "yerta" was a wider realm for travelling and sharing with other family groups. Kaurna elder Uncle Lewis O'Brien told me that he's noticed that caravan parks are often on dreaming trails, and it makes sense, they are usually close to water, and on good flat sites for camping – he calls the phenomenon our "Caravan Dreaming".

This caravan park seems edgy. The single men in the cabins look like they're on the run. I guess that's what I look like too, with my beanie and backpack and no car. Just down from my hut, a domestic dispute is in full voice.

Two leaves
in a whirlpool,
a man and a woman arguing.

By the toilet block
a hissing goose guards a caravan.
Another goose sits inside.

A cabin full of mosquitos –
sleep
is the hardest one to catch.

A storm in the night,
lightning and hail.
I edge my bed from the rattling window.

The neighbour leaves at dawn
and we all know it –
loud exhaust and transmission stuffed.

Coffee and oranges in morning sun.
A one-horned white goat
browses the green river terrace.

Leaving Cudlee Creek Caravan Park, I pass the sodden campsites of the long-term tenants by the river. Where walking by the stream is impossible, I go hand over hand, clinging to the posts behind the barrier rails on the road. Cars pass, and their drivers give me strange looks. One stops to ask if I'm alright. How to explain? I say I'm "sketching" and hold up my notebook.

There is something foreboding in the landscape here; gloomy long leaf box and manna gums along the ridges, stone walls and grey scree in the gorge, the shadowy, bluestone pools.

Down by the bend near the bridge, I've arranged to meet Bryce Bell. We'll call him "keeper of the waters", with his tattooed arms and thirty-nine years working for the water board. He unlocks the reservoir gate for me, and I continue following the river on the Old Gorge Road until it is submerged in the waters of the Kangaroo Creek Reservoir.

At last, escape from the cars. I walk through a dark green forest of broom, the river forming a large reed bed, through which the wind hisses with an ancient sound.

Following a disused road feels like walking into both the past and the future. I think of FC Holdens, round-eyed and finned, hugging the corners, and even longer ago, traps and sulkies clip-clopping through these hills. Simultaneously, I imagine that in a century's time or less the new Gorge Road might come to look like this one: closed-off, rock strewn, with grass and daisy bushes pushing up through its eroded bitumen.

Sheer, moss-covered walls –
ears open
for fresh stone falls.

On my left where a little tributary comes in, I pass the scant remains of a hut. Behind it, a feral quince tree astonishes the creek with bright orange-yellow leaves. They fall and lie still on the surface of a tannin-stained pool.

A sheep's skull
and a fallen bridge.
I hurry my step.

Now the Torrens becomes a broad stream with rapids. Bryce told me it is used as a natural pipeline, carrying drinking water into Adelaide. By opening electric valves at the foot of Kangaroo Creek Reservoir, water is sent cascading downstream to the Gorge Weir, and then via an aqueduct and tunnel into the Hope Valley Reservoir. We are still drinking from this river.

The surface of the road becomes muddy, printed with animal tracks. Beside me, firetail finches shoot in and out of luxurious sedge.

An ornate, arched bridge comes into view, its walkway coated with mud and grown over with weeds and moss. Like something from Atlantis, its surfaces have a washed and abraded feel, and parts of its railing have toppled into the creek below. And then I realise it is an underwater bridge and I am now on an underwater road, or I would be if the reservoir was full. On a block of stone someone has written the gnomic inscription, "More like existence".

Crossing the bridge and thinking of Ozymandias, I am switched to the right bank of the river. The reservoir proper begins. The river falls asleep and dreams in captivity.

Dark brown swallows
skim their own
dark brown reflections.

The hills are smudged with mist. White goats track the distant ridges and apart from the rhythmic squelch of my feet, the cry of the wood ducks is the only sound.

Loch light;
grey blends
into grey.

On the far left, Kangaroo Creek comes in. Sometimes the road is no more than a ribbon of everlasting daisy bushes, dead now in winter, but holding their form. At other times, I look down at my feet and the mosses and weeds are like corals and underwater plants and I can imagine myself walking on the bottom of a lake.

Around a bend, I meet four young men wearing hoods. They are sitting together at the edge of the forest. A primitive fear crosses my mind; I'm at their mercy. But they are as relieved as I am when I say hello and they answer in a friendly way.

To them, I must have looked like a reservoir security guard in my blue coat. They want to know about bush walks and I tell them I'm headed to the sea along the river.

The road is going steadily down and I am slipping in mud. My shoes are caked and heavy in the lifting. Then, the end; the path goes under the water, the sound of lapping all around.

The dam wall is in sight but I can't reach it from here and must cut back up through the forest to the new Gorge Road. I come to an abandoned viewing area for the reservoir. The outline of a burnt-out car is scorched onto the ground. The memorial plaques have been ripped away and the brickwork kicked over. The graffiti says "Duc 900", "Sammy Boy, R.I.P. Legend", "Red Alert – Insane Clown Posse", "Love Life", and "Slap Nuts".

There is something Pharaonic about reservoirs; their concrete and rock magnify us, make us as high as the gorge is deep, and as heavy as the mountain. I get the sense that they will be our pyramids, outlasting our civilisation. Avoiding looking over the edge, I walk along the top of the dam wall to view the spillway, that giant slippery-dip of concrete.

Empty now, its floor is strewn with massive bleached tree trunks, like sticks in a drain.

On the downstream side, at the foot of the dam wall, there is an unmoving inky pool held in a concrete chamber. Beside it, the white roar of escape and chaos as the outlet pipe discharges into another chamber and from there into the stream. A cormorant watches from the rail. I climb down the metal steps and head off with a sense of freedom, going downhill with the released water.

The sun warms the right side of my face. Monarch butterflies, with their stained-glass wings of black and white and brown, mate in the air above me. Soursobs and Salvation Jane are flowering on the shale outcrops. The stream is an always-superb composition of chance; smooth water and riffles, crimson heath by pale green rock, the beauty of the un-modelled.

Basho said, "go to the pine if you want to learn about the pine". I stop in front of a tall blue gum. Mauve, grey, white-ochre, slate-blue; so many colours exist in a square metre of its smooth bark. The base is roughed up, scarred like a Kiefer painting.

Half way up the trunk I see a sphincter from which go back and forth native bees – as in a Dali.

I could spend all day looking at the artwork of one tree. At this rate, it will take me five hundred years to reach the ocean.

High on the ridge on the way into Castambul there is a building that looks like a Venetian fort, a folly with pointed arches and battlements. In the hamlet itself, date palms grow behind an old stone house.

When I say "Castambul" I think of that tin pan alley song "Istanbul was Constantinople, now it's Istanbul, not Constantinople", and sure enough, the name is Turkish. It all comes back to the goats – maybe the ancestors of the ones I saw on the slopes earlier. In 1870, Price Maurice, a stockbreeder and pastoralist who owned land here, imported Angora goats from Kastambul, in Anatolia, south of Inebolu on the Black Sea. I've seen him in an old photograph: portly, bearded and wearing a fez.

I pass Bachelor Road, a lonely-sounding place where they once mined gold. Now it leads to lemon orchards, strawberry farms and the Mawson Trail. Tall blue gums on the hill, a perfect song room for the magpies. Silver leaves of the olives, their small fruits tinged from green to purple. Quiet kangaroos browsing.

At Corkscrew Road the Sixth Creek comes in on the left. It brings good clean water from the hills, water you can see through, to the sepia and gold pebbles on the bed. Rushing under the road, it meets the Torrens and pushes a bright wedge into the muddier river, seeming to make the ripples go opposite to the flow, but then they sweep off to the west together, down and round the bend.

The tributaries of the Torrens numbered First to Sixth Creek are like fingers on a mutant left hand, joining the brown wrist of the river. They didn't always have such anonymous titles. Colonists who planted themselves in the gullies, also laid their names on top of the creeks: Greenhill, Hallett, Todd, Anstey, and Ormsley. There are even older names for Anstey Creek: "Moriatta", or "Morialta", depending on which source you go to. Some say "Moriatta" is an aboriginal word for "ever-flowing", others that "Morialta" is a combination Kaurna word of "mari" from the "east" and "yertalla" - "flowing water" or "cascade". Names and languages are deposited, morphing identity the way sediment morphs the banks of a river.

There is a good rushing flow here and the river forms rapids and small cascades over fallen tree trunks in the course. The walking is easier now. Coots scramble away from my footsteps. Water

drips down the walls of the cutting where the road hugs the river. Bees work in yellow and cerise grevillea.

It's only by walking through a place that I can know it well. Driving is too fast for thorough perception. Car windows distance me like a film, and even if the film is watched many times, I feel like I never get onto the set. The act of walking also helps to put words together, as if the feet made sentences as well as miles.

I pass chained and meshed cliffs, wrapped like a Christo sculpture in shrouds of wire. A barred cave holds no hermit, but a pipeline coming through the belly of the mountain. Quarry trucks boom and rattle past, pushing wind in my face.

Hidden, up high,
a kookaburra scoffs
at docile realities.

Invader plants thrive by the stream: bamboo, blackberry, the bare winter limbs of ash trees, painted cadmium-yellow with lichen. Castor oil plants stand out as alien umbrellas on the bank – their seeds hold ricin, the poisoner's secret.

Some of the feral plants are more attractive – clumps of jonquils, fragrant, six-petalled white stars, with centres the colour of citron tarts.

Perhaps it's these flowers or perhaps it's the ash trees and the steep hills that make me think of Wordsworth's "The Prelude":

> The brook and road
> Were fellow-travellers in this gloomy pass,
> And with them did we journey several hours
> At a slow step …

"The Prelude" is a forty-year walk through different countries and times and all the changes in Wordsworth's thinking; an ecology of mind from nature-roving boy, to supporter of the French Revolution, to conservative laureate, taking the Queen's shilling.

In *Fugitive Writings,* Hazlitt described Wordsworth's walking style and contrasted it with Coleridge's. "Coleridge has told me that he himself liked to compose in walking over uneven ground, or breaking through the straggling branches of a copse-wood; whereas Wordsworth always wrote (if he could) walking up and down a straight gravel-walk, or in some spot where the continuity of his verse met with no collateral interruption."

Interruptions, random finds, are what I like about a walk. The river forms a cascade over white outcrops of stone then swirls either side of a little island of reeds and gum tree saplings to form a large pool. Mating cries of grebes and marbled frogs echo round my footsteps. Native pine and yacca hold on to sheer black cliffs above.

A little further down, plastic bags of rubbish, oil cans, old refrigerators and mattresses have tumbled into the stream. Creeps pull up in cars, look around quickly and throw their refuse down the banks. Our drinking water filters through their ignorance and contempt.

I arrive at Gorge Weir. A lot of trouble began here in 1860 for the purple spotted gudgeon, the river blackfish, and the mountain galaxias, their seasonal migrations up and down stream stopped by the high wall. The Torrens pours over the blocks of stone and heads on past Ambers Gully. Rain clouds, looking like ripples of sand in the sky, gather over Black Hill. A pair of sulphur-crested cockatoos are white flags, flapping against the oncoming storm.

After Gorge Weir, near where a box-girder bridge carries a water pipe over the stream and into an aqueduct, the Linear Park begins. No more roads for me. I can walk another thirty-five kilometres to the sea on a trail for bikes and pedestrians and dogs. This is the mark of a good city; being able to walk through it, without meeting a car.

The suburbs begin; I can see over the top of the riverbank the wooden skeleton of a new roof, and then a whole field of them. The place names turn Scottish and English: Athelstone, and Highbury. I travel the right bank of the river. It's late winter. Up ahead, an almond tree blooms in a patch of sunlight – early, sweet, and brave. It makes me remember daring to ask my first girlfriend out, and those words of Neruda:

> I want to do with you what spring does with the cherry trees.

The dry-stone wall covering the old Hope Valley aqueduct looks more ancient than it is, half-submerged in grass and clumps of orange-flowered Chasmanthe. A superb blue wren in his Sturt football club colours hops from stone to stone. At Wicks Estate, galahs are working the seeds from the she-oak's miniature grenades.

The river is fringed with common reeds, their fluff of dirty blonde hair catching the light. The reeds chatter and whisper and tremble like something under the water is shaking their lives – they clamour, making a susurrus like an excited city crowd, and they filter the onward stream.

The way sweeps uphill and I follow the cool smell of the path through a pine and olive grove. At the top, I look back with a sense of being released from the hills onto the beginnings of the floodplain. Below, in a beautiful left-curving pond, coots and dusky moorhens set up their contrapuntal territorial music.

This was the land of market gardens, now growing houses. Looking over the Highbury bank, I see new colour-bond and tiles, a crop of pseudo heritage and mock Tuscan estates, with names like Majestic Grove and The Dress Circle.

Coming down again to a ford on the old bullock path through the valley, I reach Helstone Mill, made from rock cut out of the banks of the Torrens. When the river was too low to drive it, the mill was wind-powered by a set of sails on the roof. Some say it gave its name to Athelstone – "At Helstone", others that the place is named after Athelstane in Scotland.

The bulrushes wave their big cigars, their wands of fuzz, and the common froglets set up their ratchety industry. A purple and red swamphen is surprised out of hiding. The river doglegs and I pass what looks like the ruins of an ancient temple high up on the left. Nothing so Romantic – it is only the blocky remnants of Fry's stone quarry. In the distance, I see the first glimpse of the city's modest towers.

Winter in our part of the world is a brief for maximum expression: the wattle's pungent yellow, the hardenbergia's violet splashes. The imports bloom as well, plum and almond speaking a kind of Japanese. Under a footbridge, the merry voice of Fifth Creek comes in. Clear and fast, the rill has an excited babble, like a three year old seeing ducks or whatever was hidden by the next bend.

After the steep banks and broad pools of Athelstone and Highbury, I am heading to Paradise. That name has always intrigued me. In my imagination, the illuminated destination board of the bus to Paradise turns the driver into some kind of archangel, and the passengers into departed souls. The name does go back to Eden. Joseph Ind created a garden here in 1854, which he called "The Garden of Paradise on the Torrens".

Outside the retirement home
ibis graze the grass banks –
step by step, closer to Paradise.

Basho was forty-five years old when he started on his *Narrow Road to the Interior,* and he already felt old and frail. He had only five years left to live. His journey through the places and the poetry he loved, was a farewell.

I make a little detour from the Torrens here, walking up Silkes Road to visit the market garden of Antonio and Lucia Parletta. For close to fifty years, they have been working the good soil deposited by the river. Lucia mostly stays inside now, but Antonio who is eighty next birthday, still tends the garden every day. Whenever I drive along Gorge Road I look for him, almost always seeing him there in his vegetable rows. Over the years, their old house has been demolished, their new one built, and their garden has shrunk as the modular estates have gone up all around. Antonio keeps only half an acre now, appearing more and more like a gardener from a parable.

Today, as usual, I find him in the garden, hoe in hand. He wears a short-sleeved shirt, fawn corduroy trousers and a floppy tennis hat covering a full head of white hair. Mud and weeds are caked to the soles of his boots. Walking slowly, he trails blades of grass through blades of grass. I think of lines by Whitman:

> I bequeath myself to the dirt to grow from the grass I love,
> If you want me again, look for me under your boot soles.

His eyes have green fractures in the pupils and he has the round, lumpy hands of decades of physical work. He is cutting cos lettuce with a long knife. His youngest daughter who is visiting calls out to him, "You don't have to keep doing this Papa." Antonio replies, "What else should I do, jump into my grave?"

Capsicum, celery, broad bean, fennel, garlic, onion and chicory in various states of growth, surround him. The sticky black soil makes the vegetables sweet, he says. Next to his chook pen, bamboo canes are neatly stacked, waiting for next summer's tomatoes. The bare fig and mulberry trees are pruned. From his eight olive trees, he makes forty-five litres of oil each year. His tractor and plough are parked under the house.

Inside, Lucia prepares lunch: pasta with tomato and chilli, a winter salad of endive, spring onion, orange, fennel and lettuce – everything grown here. The pork sausage is made at home, as well as the sweet and rough Grenache wine. While we are eating the fried sausage, Lucia sings out in her San Marchese dialect:

> carna de porcu,
> n'gauda e mena m'occa!

Rougly translated as:

> Meat of the hog,
> Cook it up and put it in your gob!

Married by proxy, they were both born in San Marco dei Cavoti in the Benevento region. Antonio came here first in 1953 and Lucia followed. As well as their crops, they raised five children in the market garden. Antonio and Lucia continue to set their lunch table every day with a cloth and have a proper meal together, primo and secondi. After good strong coffee in little cups of gold and white, I say my goodbyes and head back to the river.

t Paradise wetland, I see a great egret standing in a pool. This large white bird looks like it has escaped from a Chinese painting:

The great egret
and its reflection –
a bow aimed,
not trembling.

As I walk along the Linear Park, musk lorikeets and New Holland honeyeaters are busy in the green-tinted cream blossom of the gum trees. Beside me, a dusky moorhen makes a brief, frantic run on top of the water. Pigeons wheel over disused market gardens, up and over the soursob fields and the black branches of unpruned fruit trees.

Planning for the Linear Park began in 1979 as a flood mitigation scheme to build up the banks of the Torrens, enlarge its channels and to remove sharp bends, whilst preserving the bed of the river. Two architects with famous names, Christopher Wren and Ted Dexter, came up with the idea of a long, skinny park from the hills to the sea, and Robert Bok and David Farwell were the project managers.

I travel on the left bank of the river, looking into suburban back yards with their Tibetan prayer flags, satellite dishes, and camellias and roses trained on arches and gazebos. There never seems to be anyone home.

I cross under the Lower North East Road Bridge, heading towards Campbelltown, Windsor Gardens, Felixstow, Marden – named by property owners dreaming of England. Dernancourt though, is French in origin. The original Dernancourt, a village in the valley of the Ancre, was completely destroyed in the First World War. After the war, the people of Adelaide adopted the town, sending money and clothes, and placing its name here on the right bank of the river. Walking through, I think of Wilfred Owen, and lines he wrote about a battered statue of Christ near the Ancre:

> One ever hangs where shelled roads part.
> In this war He too lost a limb …

The river meadows are a deep rich green. Today feels like spring – a warm wind from the north makes the she-oaks sigh, and wind-chimes sing on back porches. This is the Kaurna time of Willutti; the season of moving out from the shelter trees in the foothills and uplands, down onto the plain and towards the coast, anticipating good summer fishing and hunting in the dunes and reed-beds.

Under the booming girders of Darley Road Bridge, welcome swallows build their mud nests. Mothers with prams, old couples with dogs, cyclists singly and in pairs go past with a nod.

Flannelette shirt, long white socks,
and two strapped-up knees –
the seventy year old jogger.

After Darley Road, the Torrens goes through a broad stretch then narrows to a race you could jump over with a decent run-up. It has never been a consistent watercourse. Even before all the dams and weirs and pipelines were built, it often failed to earn the title "River". In the summer of 1838, the *Register* reported that the running water of the Torrens "may be spanned with the hand, and sounded with the forefinger".

On the left, stout Scottish architecture has been laid down near this antipodean creek. It is Lochend, the stone house of Charles James Fox Campbell who gave his surname to this suburb. The restored house sits behind steel picket fencing and barbed wire to keep the vandals out, but this makes it look like a high security prison. Further up, is the foreboding two-storey Hobbs House, once a reformatory for boys, now a "behavioural intervention service". All around, the bulldozers are at work, digging the wetland ponds for the Lochiel Park Green Village development. On the opposite bank, in the caravan park, the grey nomads stake out their annexes, unfold their chairs, and read their newspapers in the sun.

I come to the Felixstow trash rack:

Down there in green water
a vandalised pay phone –
press coin return,
or follow on.

A child's pushbike
emerges from the sleep of mud,
its wheel turning
in currents of happenstance.

The trash rack is a library
stocked with wordless books,
saying who we are,
what we value and forget.

Angling in from the left, Fourth Creek runs clear through old willows to the Torrens – Moriatta joins Karrawirra Parri. I continue under stands of tall swamp-oak, the spring wind sighing through.

In a broad pool at Drage Reserve, the ducks are massing for bread thrown by picnickers: chestnut teal, wood duck, Pacific black duck and the imported mallard. I envy the way they ride downstream on the current, just using their feet to steer.

Rising at Norton Summit and Horsnell Gully, then making its way down through Magill, Tranmere, Firle and Felixstow, Third Creek comes in through a silt trap and a trash rack, entering the river as a clean cascade down rocks at the base of the O.G. Road Bridge.

Beside the bridge, on the Klemzig side, two rosellas clean their beaks using the bare twigs of a willow like a whetstone. The willow is so broad and tall, it was probably a sapling when those Old Lutherans led by Pastor Kavel first came here and named the place after their Prussian home. Words changed everything in their lives. Their refusal to use the new German state forms of worship led them to sell up and leave for the other side of the world. In the long term, we are all migrants: I with my roots in the Orkneys, that Sudanese woman waiting for the bus on O.G. Road, looking out at this new, beautiful, but strangely quiet place.

I follow a sweeping bank of soursobs, almost too dazzlingly yellow in the sun, down into the shadows of the O-Bahn underpass. A bus goes over my head with a whispered moan. The Torrens is a river of dark and light; a mixture of death and leisure, sex crimes and family picnics.

I walk through a grove of round-leafed wattle and river bottlebrush. In a secluded spot, a woman's maroon silk underpants have been left on the grass. What is the story here? Stolen from a clothesline, or a liaison sur l' herbe, or something else?

The racket of the frogs is slowly drowned by the approaching roar of Lower Portrush Road. Near the bridge, the children from Vale Park Primary school have planted wallaby grass and prickly wattle for the butterflies: the yellow sedge skipper, amaryllis azure, and orange grass dart. When my son was five or six, he used to call this river "The Torrents". I remember one day as he played barefoot, turning over rocks in the stream and looking for frogs, he handed me a rusty hypodermic needle he'd found in the water.

On another visit, not far from here, we saw the head of an Egyptian queen staring out of the reeds:

Nefertiti,
stolen garden sculpture,
surreal in the stream.

I pass Levi Caravan Park on the right bank. In the middle stands Vale House and its Moreton Bay Fig tree from the 1840s. Here fox-hunts began and afterwards formal balls were held. Adelaide's ruling class danced in their gowns and jackets and watched the moonlight on the river, while the foxes they brought here bred-up and feasted on the native creatures.

I stop for a rest, finding a seat by a laughing, gossipy part of the stream. I always choose where to sit by sound as much as view. It is a useful practice to spend part of each day simply listening to water.

Heading into Walkerville, I continue past mulberry trees and along a straight stretch of river lined by tall reeds. A steep path comes down the bank from the right. Here is one of the dark places of the Torrens. On that slope this autumn, a baby in a pram escaped from the grasp of a grandmother. The pram shot over the bank and into the water, and the baby drowned. I look down into the river, as if the place itself could somehow hold an echo of the event.

Last Mothers' Day, I saw a bunch of flowers floating in the water here.

After a long, smooth, left-curving stretch, the river breaks into rapids over stone and trailing green weed. Debris in the lower branches of the trees shows just how high the river can rise. I've seen it in spate here – the excitement of its boiling pools and muscular brown water. The willows were having their hair pulled. Islands of muck, rafts of plastic bottles, bobbed and raced seawards. Ducks cleaving to the grasses on the edge paddled sideways to escape my advancing feet and were slung fifty metres down stream.

More dark histories, just around the bend:

Slept by the stream.
Homeless man's body
found in reeds.

Under the O-Bahn bridge across from Howie Reserve where Mary Harris and Hans Heysen used to set up their easels, someone has daubed "Beware the Police – Trust No-one". What is behind that cry – a verballing, a frame-up, or paranoia?

I follow the path slowly uphill towards the Transport S.A. building. A writing acquaintance, Gwen Dally, grew up near here in the 1930s. As a child, she collected watercress for her mother at two natural fords in the stream. There were sand hills on the banks, and it was a Kaurna burial ground. These sandy sections were preferred for burial sites – why dig through hard clay? Until sand mining disturbed it, the water ran clear and was full of yabbies and turtles and fish-hunting birds. Gwen learnt to swim in the Torrens; it provided the first public pools. They evolved from the swimming holes that had local nicknames: Conrad's, The Bushy, The Kangy, Mack's, The Clay, Barney's, The Bluey, T.B's, The White Winnie, Dinny Reedman's and The Starry. The Clay became the North Adelaide Swimming Club and Mack's became the Gilberton Baths.

Near Victoria Terrace, the stream makes a sharp dogleg to the left. Because of its precipitous banks and deep water, especially on the western side, this place was known for suicides. Gwen remembered from her childhood a young woman, pregnant and unmarried, who killed herself here. Stopping above the bend, I look down and wonder what loneliness and fear, what rigidities of family or society, could make a young woman think she had no other option but this.

I take the footbridge high across the river to the left bank and continue down through an avenue of pepper trees decorated with pink berries. It's like walking through a spice cupboard. Under Tennyson Bridge, pigeons roost on steel girders.

Then it's uphill again to the steep banks of Gilberton and the suspension bridge, bouncing with each step over the river. I look down on the terraces of the old Gilberton Baths. The Gilberton Amateur Swimming Club was formed in 1915 and lasted until 1964 when the community began to take more notice of water and health standards. Now there is only a memorial gate made of pebbles, a flagpole with no flag, a light fixture with no light. But the club's insignia, a red "G" in a red shield, is still here, staring out time. My neighbour Gary told me he swam here as a boy, sliding down the high clay banks and bombing into the pool. As I head off towards St Peters, I can almost hear the squeals and splashes of the vanished summer children.

Spring days, dragonflies hovering, a perfume of wisteria, jasmine and wattle on the breeze – but there is anxiety in the air as well. We haven't had enough rain. Under the grass, the earth is already hard. The river crawls along when it should be rushing. After the Gilberton baths, a low weir lets the water through its teeth, as a comb does hair.

It would be easy to miss if you just followed the river, but here, if you take a gravel path to the left, through swamp oaks and young red gums, you come to the St Peters Billabong. Spike rush and knobby club rush line the smooth waters of the anabranch, quietly reflecting the steep, ochre-tinted banks. A water rat circumnavigates its island. With its gold, brown and black fur, and long, fish-detecting whiskers, it is more like an otter than a rat. The bird life is rich: welcome swallows dip and dive, there are black and pied cormorants, dusky moorhens and purple swamphens, grebes, coots, grey and chestnut teals.

It took me three visits to see it, but there it is, peering from a pepper tree, big, hunched and shy, with a pale cinnamon breast and a tasselled cap – the Nankeen night heron.

A concert of banjo frogs echoes from the amphitheatre walls of the billabong. Second Creek emerges here from its concrete captivity, its long run underground through Marryatville, Kensington, Norwood, Stepney and College Park. Lines from Robert Frost's poem "A Brook in the City" come to mind:

> ... The brook was thrown
> Deep in a sewer dungeon under stone
> In fetid darkness still to live and run
> And all for nothing it had ever done
> Except forget to go in fear perhaps ...

Imagine if there were wide natural corridors along all the suburban tributaries of the Torrens, as well as the Linear Park. But the colonial developers were not about to give up the creeks. The original deeds transferred "from the crown to the grantee rights to all waters, ways, timbers and minerals to you and your heirs", forever and ever, amen.

I circle back to the river and head downhill into a quiet, gorge-like section. It has the feel of a Zen garden – the stillness of grey stones and reflective water. Below the Adelaide Caravan Park, a bank of

nasturtiums looks like a pointillist painting in orange, yellow and green.

A red-finned perch browses the rock shelves under the murky water. This introduced species preys on native fish eggs and fry. It is one reason for the disappearance of the purple spotted gudgeon, once common in the Torrens. By the Second World War this little native fish was becoming rare, and hasn't been found in the river since the 1960s. The Torrens was also home to the platypus, but the last sighting was in the 1930s.

A flight of stairs comes down the hill on the right. Here, last summer, another baby drowned. His mother, distracted by a phone call, didn't see the pram roll down the bank. Thinking the baby had been abducted, she ran for help, but the boy was found strapped in his pram under the water.

Passing below Hackney Road Bridge, I am coming into "Tainmundilla" or "mistletoe place", a new name for an ancient Kaurna site for ceremony, camping and burial.

150 metres west of the bridge, at the back of Botanic Park, was the infamous "Death Hole". A projecting

ledge on the south side of the river produced swirling waters and a sudden increase in depth. Combined with perpendicular banks, it claimed the lives of many inexperienced swimmers, particularly young boys. It seems so innocuous today.

I walk on a crunchy carpet of fallen swamp oak needles, then through a precinct of public sculptures. On the left bank, behind the Zoo with its rich smells and grunts and hoots and shrieks, is the site of one of the Depression camps in the 1930s. Here men lived in tents, and fished for their dinner.

Twisted paper-bark
hangs over
a half-moon, wavering.

The evening breeze sighs through the swamp oaks, and makes me think of the "Warrawarra", the Kaurna name for a medicine man or shaman who was said to be able to transform himself into a she-oak, or into water, drowning his pursuers by leading them into the river. In 1864, William Cawthorne said, "It was devoutly believed that a certain man was transformed into a sheoak tree, the one that stood a little way above the old Frome Bridge." Hopelessly over-optimistic, I look in the vicinity, but can find no trace of this tree that probably disappeared in Cawthorne's era.

At the Albert Bridge I get a view of the city skyline and the cathedral. The bridge is ornate cast iron, painted dark green, brick red and cream. Among rosettes and stylised berries of iron, it carries the City of Adelaide coat of arms and the motto "Ut Prosint Omnibus Conjuncti" – "united for the common good".

Here, one cold September night in 1996, three young men speeding on Frome Road failed to take the bend and crashed through the bridge-rail down into the black water. Trapped in their sinking car, they all drowned.

As well as giving life to generations, I wonder how many lives this river has taken. In 1920, James Robb, a water constable responsible for patrolling the banks of the Torrens, estimated that in his sixteen years of service, ninety people had died in the river from murder, accident or suicide. I had not thought it had undone so many.

The last Popeye boat for the day goes past, almost empty, innocently churning the water.

The trees planted along the river in Grundy Gardens are white poplars, their pale grey trunks incised with the names of lovers – an ancient human practice. Two thousand years ago, Ovid described how Paris carved his first wife Oenone's name in a white poplar:

> Flourish thou poplar, fed by the bordering stream, whose furrowed bark bears this inscription: "Sooner shall Xanthus hasten back to his source, than Paris be able to live without his Oenone." Xanthus, flow backward; backward flow, ye streams! Paris still lives, though faithless to his Oenone.

Newly hatched ducklings are out in convoy today, joggers run past, and young lovers from the University roll together on the lawns of Grundy Gardens. The banks of the Torrens have always been a place for romance – first kisses, secret affairs, a gay beat, sex under the cover of darkness.

On the left, First Creek enters the Torrens through a wood-shored tunnel under Frome Road. It's like staring back into the past, looking through the darkness to the semicircle of noon light and falling water at the tunnel's end. First Creek rises at the

foot of Mount Lofty, runs through Waterfall Gully, Hazelwood Park, Tusmore and Heathpool, goes underground in Norwood and Kent Town, then emerges into the daylight again to wind through the Botanic Gardens, and around the zoo.

A photograph taken in the summer of 1870 shows women sitting on the banks of First Creek in the Botanic Gardens:

Pyramids of white tulle,
melting ice creams of organza –
from this distance they look like geese.

Doctor Richard Schomburgk, the second director of the Botanic Gardens, attacked First Creek, grading the eroded banks, ripping out the tangled vegetation and re-planting with pines. His twenty-year-old daughter Antonia died of typhoid after drinking water from the creek, which in those days was infected with raw sewerage.

The University Footbridge arches over. Just to the west of here, in 1941, Max Harris and some of his fellow writers were thrown into the river by students enraged by the first issue of the modernist literary magazine *Angry Penguins.* Thirty-one years later, in almost the same place, Dr George Duncan's body was pulled out of the river. He was new to town, homosexual, and unable to swim. On the beat that night, his watch stopped at 11.07 pm when he hit the water. There were strong suspicions that members of the vice squad were responsible for pushing him in, but though charges were brought, there were no convictions, and the verdict remains "death by drowning at the hands of persons unknown".

Arms outstretched in rigor mortis
as though reaching for the unreachable bank,
Out of a black and white river
Duncan is rolled onto the grass.

I walk on through the rose gardens and down beside the rowing sheds. The long boats lie inside like giant, empty seedpods, drying on racks. I think of those generations of young rowers' bodies. An eight speeding past in fast rhythm stirs something deep in the consciousness, back to Beowulf and the Odyssey – our oar-driven ancestry.

Stopping for lunch at Jolley's Boathouse, I look down at the faded rainbow of the paddle boats, all chained up at the water's edge, waiting for the weekend.

A memory comes to me from thirty years ago of a girl and a clumsy kiss, as we churned the river on a first date: "Come in please, your time is up" – said from a megaphone on the bank. Did they really call out like that? I don't think I'm dreaming it.

A drowsy bee circles my schooner of beer, and falls into the glass:

The bee drowns in white foam,
overwhelmed by the sweetness that drew her.
I save her with the oar of my teaspoon.

I rescue her not just because I want the rest of my beer, but because I imagine myself drowning. She drags herself around my table, like a swimmer in striped bathers, exhausted by the surf. She shudders her wings, vibrating herself back to life. I don't think she's grateful – bees don't have a god, and neither do I, unless it is perhaps nature itself – the whole great swarm of energy in space.

After lunch I walk under the arches of the King William Street Bridge. Here used to occur one of the many hidden scenes that enliven this city – part of its secret life. I found out about it from my son. On summer nights, people gathered under the bridge to play music, twirl fire sticks, juggle and play hacky sack. When I saw them last summer, they looked like a spontaneous medieval fair, or moths drawn to the light. I wonder if they will be back this year, re-taking this old gathering place, re-humanising the city at night?

Emerging from the gloom under the bridge, the reflected ripples of water and the echoing thump of the tyres overhead on King William Street, I see Elder Park opening up before me. The rotunda, that lacy meeting place, was made from Glasgow wrought iron, and shipped out from the Clyde in 1882.

Elder Park will always be the true heart of Adelaide – not only because it is the traditional site for the opening of festivals, the water and fire ceremonies, the communal singing, the concerts, the protest rallies, but because something deeper runs through here – the Red Kangaroo Dreaming. A formation of orange-tinted sandstone lies under Parliament House and Festival Theatre, and runs east under Government House along North Terrace towards the Botanic Gardens. Outcrops of this sandstone were the sacred "red kangaroo rocks" – "Tarnda Kanya". They were quarried to construct Holy Trinity Church, The South Australian Company's commercial offices and the old Legislative Council building – one law was dug out for another.

Passing chiselled blocks
of orange sandstone –
thinking of red kangaroo.

On the steps of the Festival Centre I meet Kaurna elder Joe Mitchell. The first things he points out to me are the yaccas growing in their ornamental boxes in Festival Plaza. “See those – our people used to make fishing spears from the shafts, tying on a ti-tree spike with kangaroo sinew.” He stands on the north-east corner of the steps and gestures across the river – “We had big camping grounds over there. Across here at the Parade Ground and under Festival Theatre and Parliament house, were our burial places. Yeah, Parliament House was a burial ground – we had to smoke that place, down in the basement.”

He points towards Pinky Flat over on the northern bank. “My mother belongs to that land. She was Lillian Milera, a Kaurna woman who married Thomas Grayson Mitchell from Two Wells.”

We begin walking around the central Torrens Lake. I've been told that there is secret men's business concerning this river, but Joe comes right out and says it – pointing to land in front of the southern grandstand at Memorial Drive Tennis Courts.
“That's a men's initiation place.”
“Is that secret?”
“People have said it. It's out there now.”

"Can I write it?"

"Yes, but that's all I can tell you."

We cross under the Morphett Street Bridge. William Cawthorne recorded the summer burial of a Peramangk man here in the dry bed of the river. Following the path upwards again behind the railway yards we find two black swans and their four fluffy grey cygnets nibbling at the grass. Joe stops and whistles at them. "Along here has always been our meeting place, a place for romance, and for fighting on Saturday nights after the dances." His tone changes. "You know when they pushed the Aboriginals out of here we didn't just go quietly. There were shootings. The books don't tell you that."

Coming up to the back of the old Adelaide Gaol, Joe points out the "Sorry camps" – more burial grounds on the south side. Then he nods at the Gaol itself – "I did time there in cell forty-eight."

Joe had his childhood at Point Pearce, then in boys' homes at Mount Barker and Meningie. He started work at fourteen as an apprentice moulder, went to the Riverland, then came back to Port Adelaide, working on the wharves.

"I got into the wrong company. Drinking, thieving and fencing. In gaol I learned to read and write and started to research my Kaurna heritage."

We come to the weir. "This was our old swimming spot. The kids used to dive from here." Joe and I watch a water rat surface and head into the reeds. We walk over the weir to the northern side, to "Piltawodli", the possum hunting grounds. This was where the Dresden Missionary Society men Teichelmann and Schürmann built their school and cottages, long since demolished and covered now by the golf course. Teichelmann and Schürmann learnt Kaurna and taught the children in their own language. In 1840 they published their 2000 word dictionary and grammar of Kaurna, based on what they had learnt from the elders, Mullawirrraburka, Kadlitpinna and Itymaiitpinna.

Teichelmann noted that for the Kaurna,

> the Burka – the old males, are the leaders but they have no such thing as a king or premier. They will not become servants to masters. In their view, the whites are pinde meyu "men of the grave" who should go back there after visiting, but since they do not go back, but

> permanently set up on Kaurna land, they owe food and housing to the people without the exchange of labour.

A group of pinde meyu tow their golf buggies past us along the fairway. Joe and I retrace our steps. He tells me of Kaurna burial sites west of the weir. It is part of his job nowadays to conduct proper reburials when aboriginal bones are dug up in excavations. Joe is a strong, proud man. We share a coffee together back at the railway station before he catches a train home to Elizabeth, and I head out again on my walk.

Coming down the steps to the river, I see the daylight moon is a faint thumbprint over the trees. In 1841, Teichelmann wrote of the cosmology of the Kaurna:

> It is their opinion that all the celestial bodies were formerly living upon earth, partly as animals, partly as men, and that they left this lower region to exchange for the higher one. The first celestial body that left this earth was the moon, who is considered to be a male; he persuaded all the rest to follow, that he might have companions. The sun is his wife, who beats

> him every month that he shall die; but in dying he revives again. Besides this he keeps a great number of dogs for hunting, which have two heads but no tail. The Pleiades are girls, gathering roots and other vegetables; The Orion are boys and are hunting.
>
> They say the milky way is a large river, along the banks of which reeds are growing, the dark spots in it are water lagoons, in which monsters called "yura" are living, the white clouds near the milky way are the ashes of a species of paroquets ...

The Kaurna called the Milky Way "Wodli parri" – "house river", or "home river", and considered the stars at its edge to be campfires. Before colonisation, at night in these prime hunting and fishing grounds, the central Torrens must have looked celestial – the lights of many campfires amongst the red gums along its banks.

Travelling west beside the Torrens lake, I pass the old mooring place of the Floating Palais. The ballroom with its chandeliers and second-story observation deck could hold 700 dancers doing the slow-slow, quick-quick, over the dark water. Alcohol was banned, but some of the musicians and patrons tied bottles on strings and dangled them over the side of the pontoon, keeping their booze cool and hidden. The Palais sank into the ooze in 1929 – whether due to sabotage or insurance fraud was never proven.

By Pinky Flat I meet one of the river's characters – The Swan Man. Round and bald as a Buddha, he wears a lilac Hawaiian shirt with pictures of himself and his adopted black swans and the words "Peace on Earth" sewn onto it. He is sitting on the grass, next to his bags of sliced white bread, with a group of five or six swans. One of the birds sits in his lap, and he strokes its long black neck up and down as he feeds it. The Swan Man tells me he spends three hours every day feeding and massaging the birds and that if he lies down, they will even go to sleep on him.

Pinky Flat (the north bank of the Torrens near the Morphett Street Bridge) has two possible sources for its name. Some say it comes from the Kaurna "pingko", meaning a small burrowing animal with a white tail (probably a bilby.) Bilbies, also known as "pinkies" were once common here. The other derivation comes from the 1930s when unemployed men lived in camps at this location. They drank cheap alcohol called "pinky" – an immature red wine, sweetened with sugar and boosted with whatever raw spirits they could find.

The depression camps were more extensive than just Pinky Flat. They also ran on the south side of the river, from Morphett Street to the weir, then switched to the northern bank on what is now the golf course. The men's huts were built of canvas, scraps of tin, and hessian bags. Sometimes the hessian was painted on the outside to resemble bricks and whitewashed on the inside – poverty's trompe l'oeil. The camps lasted from three to six years, and a number of the men didn't want to leave when the Depression was over. Their huts had become established homes, with fireplaces built from bricks and pug scraped from the banks of the river. The men kept dogs and tended gardens, growing tomatoes, melons, potatoes, onions, and even strawberries, watering them by carrying buckets to and from the Torrens.

Today, as I walk under Morphett Street Bridge, dragon boat races are in progress. A lizard watches me from the edge of the boardwalk:

Gold and green water skink –
the river's in
your nervous skin.

In 1906, under this bridge, the lower half of a woman's body was found floating in a sugar bag. The crime became known as the "Habibullah murder". Onlookers brought picnics and watched from the banks while the police dragged the river for the top half of the woman, which they eventually found in another sugar bag by the weir.

Here too was where the water sellers filled their iron carts in the early days of the colony. For one shilling a load, people purchased water that the more careful consumers then strained through muslin and boiled before drinking. Beer was a much safer bet. Reticulated water arrived in the colony with the opening of Thorndon Park reservoir in 1860, but even so, in 1877, the death rate in Adelaide from dysentery, typhoid and cholera was worse than in London.

In only forty years the new arrivals had turned the Torrens into a sewer and a drain for tanneries and slaughterhouses, despite the river being the main source of drinking water. Ignoring their own pollution, some colonists even wrote to the newspapers complaining about Aboriginals dirtying the water near the bridge by swimming and fishing. Until the turn of the century, Kaurna women continued to dive here for freshwater mussels.

The artificial Torrens Lake was created to beautify or perhaps anglicise the river. In 1881, 40,000 people, almost the entire population of Adelaide at the time, attended the inauguration of the weir. John Langdon, its designer, was later crippled when trying to free the jammed gates in the floods of 1889. I have met people who have said they would like to blow-up the weir, to return the river to its natural state. In the reed-beds near the gates, I hear the clamorous reed-warbler:

Bird unseen, but so present.
Singing louder than
the chiming of trains.

Just below the weir there is a pool that must contain plenty of fish. I see black cormorants lined up like a row of sailors on deck, watching the water. Three long-necked tortoises appear and slip away in the pool, just their nostrils above the surface. Positive signs. I follow black, rough-barked peppermint box trees down to the railway bridge. Nestlings in the iron girders hear time-tabled thunderstorms. On Bonython Lake, the pelicans sail.

The olive grove behind the Police Barracks looks so picturesque now, but it was where the night-soil carters dumped their loads of human excrement. It seeped into the ground water and along with blood discharged from the Thebarton slaughterhouse, joined the river, flowing to the inner western villages. Governor Hindmarsh named the waterway after Robert Torrens, chairman of the colonisation commissioners. I wonder what Torrens thought of his namesake at the time? The novelist Anthony Trollope, visiting Adelaide in 1871, said, "anything in the guise of a river more ugly than the Torrens would be impossible to either see or describe …"

Below the second weir, I pass an island of willows. In my own mind I call this the "circus bend". Over the years, in the park above, I have seen elephants and donkeys and camels tethered, and the circus

tents come and go: Ashtons, The Moscow Circus, the high architecture of Cirque de Soleil.

Around the next sweeping bend the Urban Forest scheme has revegetated the banks with thousands of native plants: bursaria, golden wattle, hop bush, wallaby grass, hardenbergia, kangaroo apple, ruby salt bush, blue gum and green-leafed box, mat rush and flat sedge. The river runs clear.

As I walk through an avenue of red gums, the approaching traffic on Port Road sounds like heavy surf. I smell the malt from the brewery and look with a jaded eye at the Bulldogs' colours painted on top of the chimney, yet again.

Passing under the Hindmarsh Bridge, I come into the area the Kaurna call "Karra-undongga". Here was where Colonel Light's original 1836 sketch proposed that a canal from the Port River would join the Torrens.

The brewery gardens are on the left bank, full of sentiment and naïve kitsch: cast cement pelicans and flamingos, a gnome riding a kangaroo, Bambi on a rock, Vulcan in his green robe, the waterwheel and the gum tree.

I think of too-sweet ice-cream from Mr Whippy vans and generations of children standing in their pyjamas looking across to the lights of the Christmas display glittering in the hot December nights. Under the looming silver tanks of the brewery, the reindeer rock in a slow, never-moving procession. Mary and Joseph watch over the baby lying on the straw, a whale spouts in the river, a cut-out cow circles the moon, and when Vulcan jerkily brings down his hammer inside his garish volcano, the soundtrack booms and fake sparks shoot up the chimney. The lame god of the forge looks tired and faded today, having waited through three seasons for the children to return.

In the flood of November 2005, Jesus, Mary and Joseph were washed out of their manger, some of the Seven Dwarfs were drowned and Moby Dick escaped, swimming as far as Underdale. By some freak of capillary action, he spouted water from his blowhole as he rode the swirling waters through Hindmarsh, Thebarton and Torrensville. Now I walk past a man playing blues harmonica to himself as he sits by the calm stream.

On the opposite bank, under thousands of silver kegs in the brewery yard, is the site of Colonel Light's house. He moved here after his wood and reed hut near West Terrace burned down, destroying most of his papers. He called his house "Theberton", after the village in Suffolk where he was educated. "Thebarton" was a typo that lasted.

By 1839, Light was out of favour with the government and elements of society who disapproved of his living with his mistress Maria Gandy. He was also dying of tuberculosis. Although he owned the land hereabouts, his attempts at subdivision were not going well. Light sold sketches to make cash, and worried about Aborigines stealing potatoes from his garden on the bank of the river. Such were the last days of the visionary surveyor general of Adelaide. He died here in October 1839, nursed by Maria who caught TB from him and died from it herself eight years later.

Near this location last summer I walked not beside the stream, but along its dry bed:

Thinking of water,
I clatter stones on the river's bed.
A lone cicada's thirsty cry.

Those secrets I imagined to lie on the stream floor were revealed by the drought. Along the rocky way, the pebble road, were the rusted remains of a tricycle, bricks and earthenware pipes, an old cash box empty of its coins. There were broken bottles, fragments of willow-pattern and blue oak-leaf china, the bones and stinking remains of carp in the last mud holes. But I didn't find the skeleton of the Giant Carp of Hindmarsh. I've heard rumour of him in the Jolly Miller bar. He must have hidden down there in a deep pool below the graveyard, fins fanning the black water, mouth working the dark ooze.

This afternoon the water looks clean as it winds beside factories, past sawtooth galvo roofs and red brick walls with truck-sized doorways where workers gather, taking the breeze and a glimpse of daylight at smoko time. Red wattlebirds hunt insects over the stream. Things have improved since Thebarton was the home of the "noxious trades" – the melting houses, the candle works, the tanneries and fellmongers, boilers of fat and hide and bone, and the slaughterhouses, disgorging brown blood and rotten offal into the stream. But when the city takes a shower, it still washes too many oils, tars, fertilisers, heavy metals and pesticides down this drain to the sea, and in summer, algae turn the Torrens a sickly cordial-green.

The piping call of forklifts in reverse
joins the cry of the coot –
their striking minimalist Morse.

With their small parcels of land and two-roomed houses, Thebarton, Hindmarsh and Bowden were suburbs intended for the workers of the flourmills and brickworks, the factories, farms and dairies. The West Torrens Football Club was originally called "The Butchers", not "The Eagles", because of the number of slaughtermen in the team, and instead of blue and gold, they wore blood-red uniforms. I have a great affection for Thebarton, having spent some of the most creative days of my life living here in Ballantyne Street in a share-house with musician friends.

On the right bank, swamp oak and she-oak and pepper tree give way to the mottled plane trees of the Hindmarsh cemetery. The graves slope down towards the river. I stop to read a few inscriptions. I like the one that simply says "RESTING" – as though the occupant is having a quick snooze and wants to be woken up in time for tea.

I reach the South Road Bridge, the boom and roar of the dodgem trucks and B-doubles passing overhead. Under the bridge, the walls are painted with the lime green, sky blue and hot pink of graffiti – or street art, to give it another name. Someone has written on the wall "the art aint for sale, but it still aint free".

I move into the sunshine of the inner industrial west, seeing the brickworks' chimney against the skyline and hearing the hiss and rumble of compressors and conveyor belts. Near here, the famous Pug Hole can still be seen, where men dug down several stories into the clay deposited by the river over millennia, to make the bricks of Adelaide's suburbs.

On the left bank, three river red gums representing "Gratitude to the Bounty of the Land", "Peace for the World" and "Atonement with the Aboriginal Inhabitants of Australia", were planted by the council for the bicentenary. In front of each tree, plaques bearing noble sentiments have been cemented into the ground. A decade later, Gratitude is thriving, the Peace tree is thin and struggling, but Atonement has gone altogether, just a sandy hole behind the plaque.

Beside a small weir at Torrensville, the fry of gambusia mill amongst the weeds and a white-faced heron is fishing the water's narrow exit point:

The heron –
hunched over, concentrating.
An academic in a grey feather gown.

This bird is also called the "blue crane". The poet John Shaw Neilson saw it as his neighbour:

> The bird is my neighbour, a whimsical fellow
> and dim;
> There is in the lake a nobility falling on him.

A man sits by the weir with a bottle of ale, after knock-off from one of the factories near by. I nod my greetings and move on. At the end of Hardy's Road, beside industrial galvanised iron roofs and fences, the river does a 180 degree bend. Willy wagtails swoop and stall over sluggish, greasy pools, and cabbage moths worry the verges amongst tangles of nasturtiums, dock weed and fennel.

I come to steep banks before the Holbrooks Road Bridge, edged with reeds twice a man's height.

Before colonisation, the Torrens didn't run out to sea, but dispersed into reed-beds and swamps that stretched as far inland as Torrensville, north to Woodville, and south to Glenelg. An 1890 painting by James Ashton shows a system of ponds and lakes to the horizon, with flocks of waterbirds. At the coast, the river filtered under a barrier of sand dunes to return pure water to the sea. In flood, the Torrens joined with the Patawalonga and the Port River. Light wrote in his journal of 1836:

> we have this morning been looking for the mouth of the river and find it exhausts itself in the lagoons, these must either ooze through the sand into the sea, or be connected with [the Port] creek.

As well as common reeds, the native vegetation included lignum, water ribbon weed, she-oak, southern cypress, and silver banksia. From the reeds the Kaurna women wove (and still weave) spiral baskets called "tainkyedli" and the men used fibre nets for hunting and fishing. Duck eggs and the ducks themselves, yabbies, and many kinds of fish, made the reed-beds a well-stocked location for summer camping.

North and south of the reed beds were extensive grasslands of native stipia and danthonia, but these were soon over-grazed by the new hard-hoofed creatures. As well as dairy farmers, the alluvial soils drew the likes of Birdseye, Holbrooks and Hardy: market gardeners and vignerons. Then the housing developers moved in, and the drainage of the reed beds began.

As I pass under the Holbrooks Road Bridge I begin to hear the clanking and beeping of earth-moving equipment around what was once the South Australian School of Art at Underdale. The bunker-like concrete buildings are gone now – replaced by empty new roads, shortly to become a housing estate. As I stare across the river from the opposite bank, I think of the young artists I knew here back in the 1980s. Some of them made their names, some died, some still practise their art in obscurity between part-time jobs: Jacky Redgate, Phillip Rees, Jack Cheslyn, Fernanda Martins, Derek Kreckler, John Foubister, Kay Flugelman and Cathy Brooks …

Wind stirs the reeds and I take up the track again which becomes very narrow on the right bank, winding beside back yard fences. I look in at fig trees, chook sheds and rotary hoists hung with

washing flapping in the breeze. Now it is late spring, Jacarandas, intensely violet, come out from suburban hiding. Going down through a grove of weeping acacias, I see a family of black swans paddling in the stream. Like teenagers that won't leave home, the cygnets have now grown as big as their parents. Only the paler red of their beaks distinguishes them from their mother and father.

I pass ti-tree and swamp paper barks with their padded trunks of soft, scrappy bindings. The flowers of the paperbark made a sweet brew for the Kaurna. The river snakes and doglegs then straightens itself to go under Findon Road, where the faces of politicians flower profusely on light poles now it is election time. Downstream from the bridge, the river broadens and sparkles and the reeds talk in the wind:

Tall reeds hide the river,
but show its course –
words point to what they cannot be.

On the left bank I see the remnants of market gardens, rusted and tumble-down green-houses, windbreaks of old olive trees and prickly pears. The river begins to turn south and the breeze picks up, carrying a faint, exciting hint of salt. The grey, deep purple and salmon pink bark of the lemon-scented gums peels off in the wind and shatters on the ground.

I am walking into Fulham, a place named by John White after his native London suburb. Unconsciously or by accident, the name fits these old reed-beds – Fulham comes from the Anglo Saxon "fullen-hame", meaning "home of the water fowl". Father and son, John and Samuel White were famous ornithologists and their family mansion "Weetunga" still stands close by in the street that bears its name. "Weetunga" is an alternative spelling of the Kaurna "Witungga" – "reedy place", Language accretes, moves on, changes like a river's course. The straight becomes bent, the broad narrow, the island is fused to the bank and the bank cut into new islands. Everything is changed and reversed again.

In the *Register* of 1919, Samuel White wrote to complain that the weir and the Torrens lake were strangling the reed-beds and causing all the waterbirds to disappear. He would be happy today to see the variety of bird life in the wetlands created here eighty-eight years later. Just in the last hour of my walk today I have seen herons, ibises, black and pied cormorants, crested woodpigeons, magpies, coots, swamphens, crows, rainbow lorikeets, spur-winged plovers, black ducks and red wattle birds. At times in the last century, the Torrens would have seemed too damaged, too degraded to save, but here is proof – it is not too late.

t Breakout Creek, the river artificially broadens and straightens, and I see the sharp wings of my first seabird – a tern, though which variety I can't tell.

Here the Torrens is a "perched river", that is, beyond its banks the ground falls away below the level of the river's bed. When the water goes over the banks it can't get back in, so these western suburbs were regularly flooded from the time they were built. It took decades for something to be done about it, partly because the councils in the higher eastern suburbs refused to contribute to paying for works downstream. After intensive lobbying, the widening of Breakout Creek and the digging of a channel through the dunes to the sea began in 1934 as a Depression work scheme.

My friend Chris Hannaford told me how as a boy he used to ride the surges of Torrens flood water here on his surf ski, being pushed out to sea amongst the sticks and rubbish and even, on one occasion, in the company of a drowned sheep. He would use his paddle to swat rats that were clinging to debris. Only now does he realise they were probably native water rats, and that also, there would have been sharks nearby, waiting for a feed.

On average, about 40 gigalitres flows through Breakout Creek to the sea each year. If this water was collected and purified in wetlands (as used to occur naturally) then stored in underground aquifers, it might reduce the destruction of sea grass and lessen the need for desalination plants or further exhausting the Murray.

Near Henley Beach Road Bridge, on a path of stepping-stones across the river, a little egret stands watching me, so white, fine-plumed, and with delicate black legs as thin as knitting needles:

Wind in the feathers
of the little egret –
Snow drifts from a bank.

After the bridge, with its concrete supports fluted to resemble Doric columns – a temple to engineering – the river flats begin. Pelicans stab and trawl the water, snickering after each motion. Planes taking off from Adelaide Airport, angle into the sky. The horses quietly browse the broad grass flats and look up briefly as I go past. They have been agisted here since the Depression but their continued presence is uncertain as the wetlands are extended:

Horse, your hooves
do not belong here –
and yet, we love your form.

In 1860, locals patriotically excited by the Crimean War, formed "The Reed-beds Cavalry", to protect the city from a coastal invasion. But the Russians never landed at West Beach and the cavalry didn't have to charge up the valley to meet them.

Dotterels fly from the water's edge as I pass under Tapley's Hill Road, my penultimate bridge. Coming up a rise and looking due west, I get a glimpse of a deeper blue than the sky, a turquoise and cobalt window framed for a moment between the black limbs of the she-oaks. I'm both excited and saddened that the end is in sight, there under the twin pillars of Seaview Road Bridge.

Royal spoonbills work the shallows in a group, like fast rice-planters. On the left bank, the Apex Park wetland gives an idea of what the original reed-beds would have been like. When the council first drained the wetlands before restoring them, they removed nearly a tonne of carp, and they also found and saved a remnant population of Murray River catfish.

Rivers end their lives in the many ways people do: they make spectacular exits through rocky gorges, or peter-out into swamps and anaesthetic marshes – the deltas of unknowing. This river is corralled into a straight line of concrete, like the corridor of an old folks' home. It passes under Seaview Road, across a weir, then meets the white, over-exposed beach sand. I wish I could keep following it; it seems such a short journey in the end.

Outsize tin sculptures of pelicans watch from wooden piles. Pigeons roost on top of the last house by the river, a drab affair of cream brick and grey tiles. Silver gulls cry. I hear the eternal sound of waves and watch the seemingly eternal fishermen on the right bank, waiting for jollytail and black bream. The river makes a final kick to the north and meets the sea side-on, as if shy about it.

One last Pacific black duck, with its wonderful eye make-up, steers away from me, back upstream. The sand is smooth like the concrete edging of a curved swimming pool and sprats dart in pale blue water the colour of moonstone.